COLONSAY Elements of an Island

C000193781

CONTENTS

Scalasaig . . . . 2 - 5

Bonaveh 6

Balavetchy 7

Balnahard . . . . 8 - 13

Uragaig . . . . 14 - 15

Kiloran . . . . 16 - 21

Kilchattan . . . . 22 - 25

Machrins . . . . 26 - 27

Ardskenish . . . . 28 - 31

Garvard . . . . 32 - 35

Oronsay . . . . 36 - 39

Balerominmhor . . . . 40 - 41

Baleromindubh . . . . 42 - 43

Acknowledgments and References .44

SCALASAIG

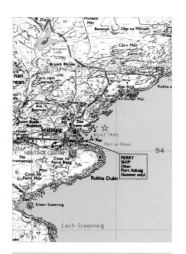

The pier towards Glassard

The harbour

An eminent Victorian geologist noted that when approached by steamer from the east side "Colonsay has a barren, uninviting appearance, the shores being rocky and often precipitous, and the prospect inland being closed by bare, rugged hills. But the interior is extremely fertile, showing wide stretches of pasture-land and good agricultural farms".

James Geikie

The Mole

Benoran

Loch an Sguid - top

The Parish Church

Port an Obain

Glassard

Dùn Eibhinn

BONAVEH

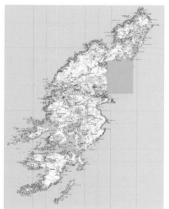

Fishing village ruins at Riasg Buidhe - abandoned 1920s

Bodach Ruadh – Codling
Gealag – Sea-trout
Langa – Ling
Liù – Lythe or Pollack

Piocach – *Saithe*; Coal-fish (Cuddy). In the young state it is known as *Cuddainn* (Cuddy); in the May following, *Céiteanach*. *Piocach* is applied to it in the second year, and *Piocach-mòr* after. *Ucsa* is the mature fish.
Rionnach – Mackerel

BALAVETCHY

Rionnach-an-Eich – Horse Mackerel
Sgadan – Herring
Sgat – Skate
Siolag – Launce; Sand-eel (local)
Sporran Feannaig – Mermaids Purse: the egg of the Dog-fish
or a species of skate
Suil Oir – Poor Cod
Trosg – Cod

Murdoch McNeill

BALNAHARD

Sgibinis

Towards Beinn Bheag and Carnan Eoin

Rubha Geodha

Port Sgibinis

Rubha Mór Nighean Eoin
Balnahard Bay - below

Port na Cuilce

Colonsay	(Total)	Balnahard
1841	979	32 people in 6 households
1851	837	40 people in 8 households
1861	598	22 people in 3 households
1871	456	5 people in 1 households
1881	395	9 people in 1 households
1891	331	12 people in 2 households

Professor John Sheets

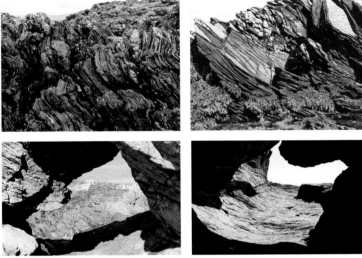

Window of Hercules - middle

Tràigh Bàn

Rubha Mór Nighean Eoin - bottom

Looking towards Jura from Sgeir Nic Fhionnlaidh - bottom

URAGAIG

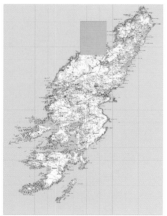

Natural arch towards Port nam Fliuchan

Achadh Téaltaig – Hut Bay Field

Aoineadh na Cailliche – The Hag's Terrace

Aoineadh Caoraich Iomhair – Ivar's (Norse name) Sheep Terrace

Aoineadh na h-Ulaiche – Treasure-trove Terrace

Blàran Boidheach – The Pretty Little Level

Bearradh an Arbhair – The Precipice with the Standing Corn

Dùn Téaltaig – Hut Bay Fort

Cailleach Uragaig – The Old Woman of Uragaig

Creag nan Ubhal – Apple Rock

Port an Tigh Mhóir – Large House Harbour

Struthan na h-Oisge – Ewe Streamlet

Uragaig – a heap of stones on the beach

Uamh an Dùnain Ghuirm – Cave of the Green Knoll

John de Vere Loder

KILORAN

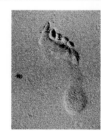

Kiloran Bay

Looking towards Eilean Meall na Suiridhe

Looking towards Uragaig from Sgibinis - top

Kiloran Bay looking towards Creagan

Loch Sgoltaire

Remains of castle

Boat house

Tucked in the shelter of Beinn an Sgoltaire, Loch an Sgoltaire is now tamed by Scottish Water to supply the needs of Colonsay's inhabitants. The islands of the lake inspire many stories, not least that they acted as the religious shelter of an Irish priest, perhaps one who accompanied Antrim's army into Scotland in the early 1600s, who now has an island named after him (Eilean Dubh Iain Mhitchel). An island fortification, originally a refuge of the MacDuffies in medieval times, is a relic of Sir James MacDonald's rebellion of 1614–15, renovated in the late 19th century and subsequently used as a summer retreat.

Tony Fox

The luxuriance of the trees in the neighbourhood of Colonsay House astonishes the stranger, who, while wandering in their glades, might easily fancy himself in some well-wooded part of the Lowlands.

Here we find growing vigorously in the open air, all the year round, several plants which on the mainland could not survive the winter.

James Geikie

KILCHATTAN

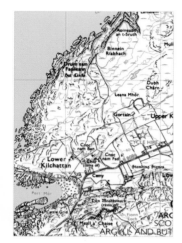

Loch Fada

Baptist Church

Cnoc nam Fad - top   Remains of Chapel - bottom

Cliffs of north coast

Garbh Chladach looking towards Port Mór

Fingal's Limpet Hammers

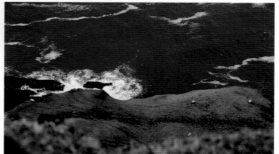

The New Loch

Loch Fada looking towards Beinn nan Gùdairean

The glassy calm of Loch Fada belies the fevered activity below the mirror surface. Being of good nutrient status, the loch supports a rich and varied flora, including the slender Naiad, a rare British submerged aquatic plant species, known from only 36 (mostly Hebridean) lochs. Loch Fada (Long Lake), in fact consists of three separate basins constituting the largest of Colonsay's water bodies. It is the summer breeding home of the diminutive Dabchick or Little Grebe, but in winter Loch Fada supports many ducks such as Goldeneye, Pochard and Tufted Duck, fleeing the cold winter conditions of their breeding grounds further north. They are joined from October to April by several hundred Greenland White Fronted Geese that feed on the bogs, rough pasture and in-by fields of Colonsay and which use the loch as a safe overnight roosting place.

Tony Fox

MACHRINS

Beinn nan Caorach

The white felspathic grits appear over scattered areas in the north-east of the island and in the Machrins group of grits and mudstones they enter into the formation of part of the hilly south of Machrins rising into Carn Chaointe . . .

Murdoch McNeill.

Dùn Ghallain

Stretching out to sea and rising abruptly from the Atlantic, *Dùn Ghallain* – named after Gallan, who was reputed to be a son of the King of Lochlann – formed an easily defended site for the fort that once crowned its summit. Flanked on either side by pretty sandy beaches – *Tràigh an Tobair Fhuair* (Cold Well Strand), on the north and *Port Lobh* (Foul Harbour), on the south.

Murdoch McNeill.

ARDSKENISH

Near Coite Creige

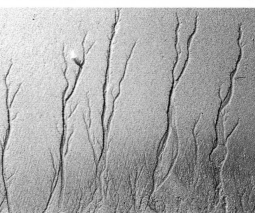

Sguid an Leanna

GARVARD

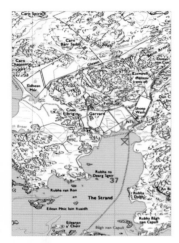

Early on a summer's day a delightful scent leaps
from every plant around your banks, as the dew rises off the heather.
The skylark sings her song to me, lightening my step,
And among the bog-myrtle the clever spider has spun its web.

Tràth latha anns an t-samhradh tha fàileadh cùbhraidh leum
Bho gach lus ma d' bhruachan, is drùchd a fàgail fraoich.
Tha 'n uiseag 's i a' seinn dhomh, ag aotromach' mo cheum,
'S measg roiteagach tha snàthainn an damhain-eallaich ghleusd'.

from "The Temple Burn" by Donald A. MacNeill

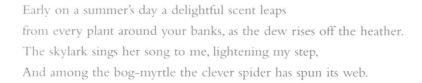

An Gleann

A slow-flowing stream – *Abhainn-a-Ghlinne* – running parallel with the base of the rocks is the home of the Water Ranunculus, the Least Marshwort, and other aquatic plants. The elegant fern-like foliage of the Meadow-rue appears here and there from clefts in the rocks, and masses of the reddish-purple Hemp Agrimony and pink-tinged Valerian grow on the banks of the stream.

Murdoch McNeill.

Poll Gorm

ORONSAY

Far, far away am I,
far away from the lovely island,
the lovely island, floating in the west,
a little jewel, forever in my heart.
Far, far away am I.

Oronsay of the sandy beaches,
beaches of fine sand, sifted by the waves,
fresh breakers from the bosom of the ocean
crashing loudly as of old.
Oronsay of the sandy beaches.

In your tranquility I was brought up,
was brought up and nursed;
warm and gentle days of summer,
running bare foot by Loch Bàn.
In your tranquility I was brought up.

'S fhada, 's fhada thall tha mise,
'S fhada thall bhon eilean àluinn
Eilean àluinn snàmh 'san iar,
Ailleagan gu bràth 'nam chridh'.
'S fhada, 's fhada thall tha mise.

Orasa nan tràighean grinneal,
Tràighean grinneal mìn gan sluaisreadh,
Stuadhantan ùr bho uchd a' chuain
Bualadh fuaimneach mar o chionn.
Orasa nan tràighean grinneal.

'Sann 'nad thàmh a fhuair mi m'àrach,
Fhuair mi m'àrach òg is m'altrum.
Làithean samhraidh, maothach, blàth,
Casruisgt' ruith mi taobh Loch Bàn.
'Sann 'nad thàmh a fhuair mi m'àrach.

from "Far Away Am I" by Donald A. MacNeill

Eilean Ghaoideamal towards Jura - top

Seal Cottage

BALEROMINMHOR

Many a wonderful thing we saw while at sea:
small seals like sheep on the rocks, fast asleep;
a black cormorant - the great fisherman - searching the waves,
and kittiwakes screaming above our heads.

Gur ioma nì prìseil a sheall sinn air cuan:
Ròin bheaga mar chaoraich air creig, 's iad 'nan suain;
Sgarbh dubh, an sàr-iasgair, a' sgrùdadh 'sna tuinn,
Is sgàireag nan creag le sgread os ar cionn.

from "Boyhood Days With My Father" by Donald A. MacNeill

From Port a' Chapuill towards Paps of Jura

BALEROMINDUBH

Lacha Mhor – Eider Duck
Known in neighbouring islands as Lacha Cholasach (Colonsay Duck)

Loch Cholla - top

Murdoch McNeill

Baleromindubh Bay

ACKNOWLEDGMENTS

This book would not have been possible without the help and co-operation of many people, in particular the islanders who have allowed me to walk (and climb) freely across Colonsay and Oronsay. Specifically, I would like to thank the following: Bradford College, which, in the form of 'staff development', gave me encouragement and support throughout this project – my teaching will benefit from this experience; John Stainton for his computer expertise, tolerance and advice; Tony Fox and Dr. Ruth Brompton for their good words; Anne Needham for the trial loan of equipment; my family in their 'concern' for the many trips I have made to the island; and also friends, colleagues and students.

Finally, it is evident that my publishers have been superb in their enthusiasm and guidance, especially Georgina Hobhouse. I also know how vital a part, both Kevin and Christa Byrne play, in the life of Colonsay. It has been an inspiration to make this record and I hope it will provide others with an image of the island that they will treasure.

Brian Hindmarch – July 2003

REFERENCES

McNeill, Murdoch, *Colonsay One of the Hebrides*, Colonsay, House of Lochar, 2001

MacNeill, Donald A., *Moch is Anmoch*, Colonsay, House of Lochar, 1998

Geikie, James, 'Notes on the Geology of Colonsay and Oronsay', *Transactions of the Geological Society of Glasgow, 1878-79*

Loder, John de Vere, *Colonsay and Oronsay in the Isles of Argyll*, Colonsay Press, 1995

Sheets, Professor John, 'Economic and demographic consequences of population decline: Colonsay and Jura, 1841-1891', *Northern Scotland, Vol 6, No 1*, 1984

Colonsay & Oronsay, Explorer 354
Reproduced by permission of Ordnance Survey on behalf of The Controller of Her Majesty's Stationery Office
© Crown Copyright, Licence number 100013374

    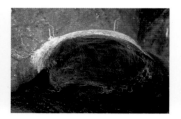